RASTA • IS • CUSS

A • DICTIONARY • OF
RASTAFARIAN • CURSING

Other Masalai Press Books

- *One Thousand One Papua New Guinean Nights: Folktales from Wantok Newspaper. Volume 1: Tales from 1972-1985.* Edited and translated by Thomas H. Slone. 528 pages, 8-1/4 by 11 inches. ISBN 0–9714127–0–7.
- *One Thousand One Papua New Guinean Nights: Folktales Stories from Wantok Newspaper. Volume 2: Tales from 1986-1997, Indices, Glossary, References, and Maps.* Edited and translated by Thomas H. Slone. 613 pages, 8-1/4 by 11 inches. ISBN 0–9714127–1–5.
- *Prokem: An Analysis of a Jakartan Slang,* by Thomas H. Slone, 108 pages, 5 by 8 inches. ISBN 0-9714127-5-8.

RASTA • IS • CUSS

THOMAS • H • SLONE

PUBLISHED • BY
MASALAI • PRESS
OAKLAND • CALIFORNIA
2003

Published by
MASALAI PRESS
368 Capricorn Avenue
Oakland, California 94611-2058
U. S. A.

First Edition, 2003

Publisher's Cataloging-in-Publication Data
Thomas H. Slone, 1960-
Rasta Is Cuss:
A Dictionary of Rastafarian Cursing /
by Thomas H. Slone.
p.   cm.
ISBN 0-9714127-4-X

1. Rastafari movement — Dictionaries
2. Rastafari movement — History
3. Words, Obscene
4. Swearing — Dictionaries
5. Invective — Dictionaries
6. Puns and punning
I. Slone, Thomas H. II. Title

The title of this book is from a line in "A Hymn to the Concept of Ras Tafari" by Ras "T", as printed in Barrett (1988: 189-190).

I wish to thank Velma Pollard for her assistance.

Table of Contents

Introduction

Rastafarianism is a messianic and millenaristic religion (Barrett, 1988: 109-110). It developed as the result of an alleged prophecy by the pan-Africanist, Marcus Garvey that a black king would arise from Africa before Judgment Day. The founders of Rastafarianism were Jamaican followers of Garvey who recognized the coronation of the Ethiopian Emperor Haile Selassie (née Tafari Makonnen, later Ras Tafari; *ras* is an archaic word for "prince" in Amharic [Kane, 1990: 381]) in 1930 as corresponding to this prophesy. Selassie was crowned in the legendary lineage of King Solomon, further adding to their belief in his stature (Barrett, 1988: 80-84).

Though Rastafarians are today as a whole leaderless, their religion has spread to many countries. Though, they are a religious minority, they have influence beyond their numbers in Jamaica's politics, art, and language.

The basic beliefs of Rastafarians prior to the death of Selassie were:

- "Haile Selassie is the living God.
- "The Invincible Emperor of Ethiopia is now arranging for expatriated persons of African origin to return to Ethiopia.
- "The Black person is the reincarnation of ancient Israel, who, at the hand of the White person, has been in exile in Jamaica.
- "The White person is inferior to the Black person.
- "The Jamaican situation is a hopeless hell; Ethiopia is heaven.
- "In the near future Blacks shall rule the world." (Barrett, 1988, 104)

Except for the first two beliefs, these were not universally excepted, but were probably reasonably representative of those calling themselves Rastafarians (Smith *et al.*, 1978: 17, 23-24). These beliefs have changed since the death of Selassie. Most Rastafarians now accept the physical death of Ras Tafari, but still regard him as God. Unrelated to his death, Rastafarian beliefs have changed in other ways as well. Repatriation to Africa is no longer seen by all as inevitable, and most view the liberation of Jamaica as necessary before repatriation to Africa (Barrett, 1988: 172). The atti-

2

tude of many Rastafarians towards Jamaica has become less negative (see *jamdown*). The attitude towards whites is less severe than indicated in the above quote: whites have joined the religion and are treated as brethren. Whites who repent from evil behavior are considered the equals of blacks, similarly there is a recognition that not all blacks are good (see *iyabingi*). Two other aspects of Rastafarianism are also important to nearly all members: the King James Version of the Bible is used as Holy Scripture, and ganja is used as a holy sacrament.

The speech of Jamaican Rastafarians is a variant of Jamaican Creole. Jamaican Creole is an English-based creole that is a product of colonialism. The Spaniards were the first to colonize Jamaica, but had little direct influence upon development of Jamaican Creole. When British colonialists ousted them, the Spaniards' African slaves escaped into the mountains where they retained much of their African culture and some of their African languages. The British brought more slaves from Africa, but were unable to recapture the escapees, known as Maroons, and so instead maintained a negotiated peace settlement with them. The Maroons reinforced the African influences in Jamaican Creole that the British slaves brought. Maroons also influenced (though not always directly) various Afrocentric political and religious movements, including the Rastafarians. Maroon retention of African culture has generally been seen as positive by these movements despite the Maroons' agreement with the British to return all newly escaped slaves. Other aspects of the Caribbean milieu (e.g., French, Portuguese, Spanish, Dutch, Hindi and Amerindian languages) have also influenced Jamaican Creole. The most recent language additions to Jamaican Creole are primarily from the Rastafarians (Roberts, 1988: 43), who besides adding a few Amharic words, have made many linguistic innovations.

The language of the Rastafarians is known as Rasta Talk or Dread Talk by non-Rastafarians, and as *Iyaric* ("I" + "Amharic") or *Livalect* ("live" + "dialect") by Rastafarians. In Jamaica, it exists as one of a number of registers of Jamaican Creole that indicate social standing and/or situation. Rasta Talk

4

was initiated by the sect known as the Youth Black Faith, founded in 1949 (Chevannes, 1978: 173, 189-190). Nearly all Jamaicans speak or at least understand several registers of Jamaican Creole (Roberts, 1988: 82). Rasta Talk is not spoken by non-Rastafarians, but many words from Rasta Talk have entered other registers in Jamaican Creole; this is mainly due to the international popularity of reggae[1] music and its linkage with Rastafarianism. Rastafarians had little or no influence upon Jamaican Creole prior to the 1960s.

---

[1]Various origins are given for the word reggae, but Frederick "Toots" Hibbert (arguably the first reggae musician) gives the origin as "raggedy, everyday stuff." (Grass, 1982: 45) *See also* Cassidy and Le Page (1980: 504).

Rasta Talk was initially intended to be a secret language to counter societal oppression (Chevannes, 1978: 190). Pollard (1986: 157-158) explains, "It seems that the language was intended to be secret…. [ellipsis hers] This particular intention was, however, short-lived: the language of Rasta soon moved into the youth culture of Jamaica." Jamaican Creole and other creoles have themselves functioned as languages of secrecy.

"From their very inception these creole languages fulfilled a semi-clandestine function, enabling blacks to communicate with one another in the presence of whites with some measure of safety… [They did this] through the use of ridicule, subterfuge, inversion and allusion in communication, and a reliance on intonation, rhythm, contextual definitions of words and non-verbal/paralinguistic features to convey meaning, the dominant white values and racist caste definitions that were built into the slave system were challenged, broken down and recon-

stituted in a black context."
(Jones, 1988: 7)

Rasta Talk is therefore, in this sense, a re-creolization of Jamaican Creole because of its anti-colonial linguistic modifications and because of its initial secrecy. Rasta Talk still functions as a secret language despite leakage into other registers of Jamaican Creole, since urban Rastafarians live in crowded conditions among non-Rastafarians, and need to hide some of their activities, particularly ganja use (Yawney, 1979a: 148).

Numerous linguistic registers in Jamaican Creole are associated with social strata; consequently the Jamaican elite who speak standard (i.e. "the Queen's") English negatively value most of these registers. The elite has similarly thought of Rasta Talk and Rastafarianism as "low class." Rastafarians, however, do not view Rasta Talk as low class or even as a register: to them it is African, anti-colonial, and spiritual. Jamaicans (90% of whom are of African descent) have long sought after all-things European. Rastafarianism is a rejection of this Europhilia; the Rastafarians have shown, in large part due to the popularity of reggae, that things related to Africa have value.

The linguistic modifications of Rasta Talk are both numerous and dynamic. Linguistic modification is seen as a necessity by Rastafarians because Jamaican Creole is a product of colonialism and because Jamaican Creole is viewed as an inadequate vehicle for their religion. Bones (1986: 49-50), himself a Rastafarian, explains:

> "One of the key aspects of language is its role as a control mechanism. A highly restricted language is elitist in character, so it reflects all sorts of biases and prejudices. Rastas are saying that the language of the former colonial masters (say, English) is biased and prejudiced, reflecting the values and morals of the colonial masters' conduct and behaviour.... The British, for example, used their language as they used guns, money, law, religion, politics or anything else: as a weapon in the battles and wars of domination and foreign rule."

Similarly, the Kenyan writer Ngũgĩ felt it necessary to cease writing in English, the colonial language of Kenya, and to write instead in Swahili. For him, this was an act of recapturing his Africanness (Ngũgĩ, 1986). In addressing the question of the relevance of language to religion, Fell (1989: 14) states, "the problem of theological statement or God-talk is to find an adequate vehicle to communicate faith that is consistent with physico-scientific understanding." Standard English or even Jamaican Creole was therefore not an adequate vehicle of religious communication for Rastafarians. These languages represent colonialism to the Rastafarians and they did not adequately represent either the desperate poverty of the slums of Kingston, Jamaica from which many Rastafarians originate or the Ethiopia to which they aspire.

The main focus of innovation in Rasta Talk is decolonization: giving benedicta to perceived Afrocentric concepts and maledicta to perceived Eurocentric concepts. Pollard (1983: 49; 1986: 161) summarizes the various methods used by Rastafarians to decolonize Jamaican Creole:

> "Category I. In which known items bear new meanings (e.g. *chalice* = pipe for smoking ganja)
>
> "Category II. In which words bear the weight of their phonological implications (e.g. *downpress* = oppress)
>
> "Category III. /ai/ words.
>> i. Pronominal function, e.g. *I, I-man* = I; me.
>> ii. Initial syllable replacement, e.g. *I-lalu* = calaloo [k.o. vegetable]
>
> "[Category IV. In which the Jamaican Creole] meaning is not always obvious e.g., Deadahs /dedaz/ is the word for 'meat,' which is indeed the dead flesh it is regarded to be by Rastas, who are mainly vegetarians"

Rasta Talk can also be characterized as having much metaphor, homophony, puns, and verbal aggression. The use of metaphor is perhaps due to the Rastafarians' reliance on the Bible in daily life; the homophony is a consequence of its being derived from a creole (Todd, 1974: 19); and the puns are partly a result of its being derived from Jamaican Creole (Pollard, 1983: 50). Jamaican Creole is rich in puns and maledicta (e.g. see Cassidy and Le Page, 1980; Cassidy, 1982; Dance, 1985; Roberts, 1988; and Cooper 1995). But, Rasta Talk may be even richer in puns and maledicta, for "punning appeals particularly to exiles (whether external or internal)" and can often be used for verbal aggression or political satire (Redfern, 1984: 123-125, 164). It was noted fairly early in the history of Rastafarianism (1958) that "filthy language [was] perfectly in order among some brethren, who hold that no words are bad in themselves." (Smith *et al.*, 1978: 15) But, at least one group of Rastafarians forbids "indecent language" (Simpson, 1980: 219).

The verbal aggression of Rasta Talk is due in part to the Old Testament

(Smith et al., 1974: 27). For example, Edward (n.d.: 47) cites Deuteronomy 28, Moses' grand curse to the disobedient; Nicholas and Sparrow (1979: 45) cite several curses and strictures used by Rastafarians from Exodus and Leviticus; and Owens (1976: 36-37) cites a strong reliance on prophetic and apocalyptic books of the Bible. Faristzaddi (1982) further explains the reason for language transformation:

> Within the word/sound structure of the Queen's English there exist subtle negative connotations in the spelling and pronunciation of certain words. Rastafarians are continually exploring these negatives and seek to substitute and re-affirm more positive vibrations, thereby adding to the complexity of the Emperor's [Selassie's] language by altering whatever negatives can be found in the finite Queen's English. Within the words 'be(lie)f', 'bles(sin)g', and '(sin)cere' we can perceive the word-vibrations of 'sin' and 'lie.' In the case of 'sin', the 's' is dropped reaffirming the 'word,

sound and power' positively as 'Incerely' or 'Icerely.'

Rastafarianism is not only a reaction to colonialism, but to Jamaican society as well, which the Rastafarians see as being the result of colonial policies to this day.

In contrast to the Rastafarians' direct reevaluation of words, black Americans have used a process that Sims Holt (1972) calls "inversion": the exaggeration of labels for insult (e.g. calling a white army corporal a "captain") or for solidarity (e.g. black use of "nigger" [Major, 1994: 319-320]). This process has also been used in Jamaican Creole, and has often been unrecognized or misunderstood (Sims Holt, 1972: 158; Dundes, 1980: 52-54; Campbell, 1987: 22, 99). Rasta Talk and inversion are similar with regard to self-reference by negating the values of otherwise self-oppressing labels (e.g. *bungo* in Jamaican Creole and "nigger" in English), but different with regard to reference to outsiders (i.e. non-blacks). Inversion exaggerates, whereas Rasta Talk negates (e.g., *Elizabitch*).[2] Inversion in black language is part of a larger process in slang whereby values of words are frequently negated (Wentworth and Flexner, 1975: xi-xii).

The compilation that follows, lists those words and phrases which have been transformed into maledicta by the Rastafarians, rather than those that have been transformed from perceived maledicta (e.g., *Icerely*). Also listed are those Jamaican Creole maledicta, which have been used against Rastafarians. Some of these have been turned into benedicta by the Rastafarians. The compilation includes maledicta from groups which many would not consider Rastafarians (e.g., Ethiopian Zion Coptic Church and Jamaican criminals in New York City [N.Y.C.P.D., 1985]) but who call themselves Rastafarians, these are noted as such. The speech of all of these groups is consistent with Pollard's categorization of Rasta Talk, even non-Rastafarians' maledicta against Rastafarians (e.g., *Rasta clots*) is consistent, and is indicative of the influence of Rastafarianism.

---

[2] For another perspective on inversion see Dundes, 1987: 150-158.

Rastafarian maledicta focuses upon religion, politics, sex, food, and hair. Purely religious maledicta are derived from Rastafarian interpretation of the Bible (e.g., *Babylon*) and/or are directed against Christianity (e.g., *Jesus*). Religious intolerance is of course nothing new (e.g. see Hughes [1991: 91-100] for a discussion of the blossoming of religious maledicta during the Reformation). Rastafarians are both the creators of (e.g., *Pope*) and objects of (e.g., *Blackheart Men*) such maledicta.

It has often been noted that Rastafarianism is not just a religion, but a political philosophy. Political maledicta focuses upon both Jamaican (e.g., *Blind-aga*) and international politics (e.g., *Elizabitch*). International political maledicta is exclusively against British colonialists with the exception of Ulysses S. Grant (see *Four Great Pirates*) who is seen as a neo-colonialist for his failed role in the Reconstruction period of the United States.

Sexual maledicta focuses upon the historically inferior position of women in Jamaica (e.g. *clapping beef*), and upon the Rastafarian menstrual taboo (e.g., *Blood clot!*). Rastafarianism has

15

historically been a patriarchal system. This is a reaction against the matriarchal structure of Jamaican society, which is due to the colonial policies that encouraged separation of the father from the family (Kitzinger, 1969: 259-262). The shift from matriarchy to patriarchy has resulted in language modification, including words that denigrate women (*clapping beef, blood clot!, Elizabitch, pussy cloth!, skeef, Rastaman-woman, woe-men*).

Rather than use of food taboos as inter-group maledicta as is common for other groups (Clifton, 1978: 150), Rastafarians use maledicta against the food itself (*Arnold, buried food, duppy, morgue, saalting, that thing*). While *Arnold* refers directly to the food in question (meat), it also alludes to white people and is thus exceptional. Rastafarian food taboos are different than general Jamaican food taboos, but the Rastafarian focus on food is an extension of the Jamaican substrate's focus on food cleanliness (Sobo, 1993: 111-115).

Rastafarian maledicta indicates an obsession with hair (*baldhead, bald tail, bathroom locks, beardsman, com-*

16

bsome, burn head, dreadlock, nubbies, three unclean spirits). This is confirmed by Davis and Simon (1992: 115, 122) who state that *flashing locks* (unleashing *dreadlocks* [long, matted hair] from a hat or tam) is "a popular Dread pastime." This obsession is primarily because *dreadlocks* are today the most obvious (but not absolute) way of identifying Rastafarians. Black Americans and non-Rastafarian Jamaicans are also have obsessions with hair (e.g. "good hair" [straight] vs. "bad hair" [kinky]; see *head* in Johnson [1972: 148]). *Dreadlocks* are a rejection by Rastafarians of the hair-straightening obsession. Hair has a magical quality for many Jamaicans (Chevannes 1978: 160, 185-186) and this may explain why the hair obsession has been negated by Rastafarians rather than eliminated. The erection of the hair is associated with both insanity and fear (Darwin, 1965: 294-297), and this may also contribute to the negative perception of Rastafarians.

Maledicta used against Rastafarians has focused on alleged lack of hygiene (*billy goat, dirty John Crow, dutty tils, ram goat*, and *Rasta clots*) and on

17

folkloric allusions (*Blackheart Men* and *dirty John Crow*). Though Rastafarians are almost always frequent bathers, the appearance of their hair probably contributes to the folk belief that they are not hygienic.

Rastafarians have been subjected to severely disparaging descriptions and perceptions by the general Jamaican society: "'The menacing devils with snake nests for hair.' 'Cult that worships old newspaper clippings of Haile Selassie.' 'The Rastafarians — the ones who use manure in their hair.' 'No good Jamaican bums'" (Sanders, 1982: 59), "rascals, nasty, wicked, interferers, [and] curse[rs of] women" (Chevannes, 1978: 213). Rastafarians, at least historically, have come from among the poorest of the poor. Consequently, Rastafarian culture (reggae music, sculpture, language play, and religious millenarism) is a direct result of coping with poverty and oppression (Legman, 1964: 324-325; Manley, 1982: 11-13).

As with most creoles, Jamaican Creole has a plethora of orthographies, many of which attempt to match its pronunciation. With the exception of quotations, I have attempted to use the same orthography as Cassidy and Le Page (1980), the most complete dictionary of Jamaican Creole.

Word meanings that predate Rastafarianism but which are strongly associated with Rastafarians (e.g. *raas*), or that may not have originated with Rastafarians but fit into the Rastafarian system of word transformation (e.g., *Blind-aga*) are marked by a "*". The English creoles used on the various Caribbean islands differ to varying degrees, hence Rasta Talk from other islands (Barbados, Dominica and Grenada) is so noted. The Earth People are a small religious group in Trinidad, distinct from Rastafarianism. It is of interest to note that Rastafarianism has linguistically influenced the Earth People (Littlewood, 1993: 77, 244-252). Cursing is an important aspect of the Earth People religion (Littlewood, 1993: 164) as with Rastafarianism. Cursing has been carried to an extreme that most Rastafarians would find upsetting: "Fuck God!" is the Earth People's favorite aphorism (Littlewood, 1993: 109).

Dictionary

alligator ruling "We the people are tired of colonialism and imperialism, also alligator ruling." (Edward, n.d.: 21) Presumably, alligator ruling is rule by the vicious and thick skinned.

Arnold euphemism for pork. Pork is strictly prohibited for Rastafarians. "When a Rastafarian is hungry and can find nothing but the gift of a piece of pork, he will change the name to Arnold, and then partake of it." (Barrett, 1988: 140) Since *Arnold* is a purely European name, neither Africanized nor turned into a nickname, it suggests that the pork is being anthropomorphized into a white man (Dillard, 1972: 17-35). Furthermore, Ras Hu-I equates carnivorism with cannibalism, "They are cannibals. Western people are cannibals. They fill up on dead flesh to try to find the virtue of life." (Bishton, 1986: 104) The equation of carnivorism with can-

21

nibalism is made in other societies as well (Fiddes, 1991: 129-130; Tannahill, 1975: 149; Legman, 1975: 555, 558-560). See also *buried food, duppy, morgue, saalting, that thing*

Babylon / Babylon system a catch-all maledictum of Biblical derivation: the establishment, police, whites, white society, a non-Rastafarian, Jamaica, the Christian church, the Vatican (White, 1989: 332); used by some non-Rastafarian Jamaicans to describe Rastafarians (Cassidy and Le Page, 1980: 17, 491); a soldier, a wicked person, a place of wickedness (Pollard, 1982: 29); colonial and neocolonial oppression, the Mafia, the judiciary, anything non-Rastafarian (Chevannes, 1978: 4); "the North American/European power complex" (Owens, 1976: 37); the Western world; the West and the former Soviet Union (Smith *et al.*, 1978: 20). Faristzaddi (1982) and Nicholas and Sparrow (1979: 30) cite Rastafarians' main biblical reference, "Mystery, Babylon the great, the mother of harlots and abominations of the earth." (Revelation 17: 5) *Babylon System* is the name of a Wailers[3] song (White, 1989: 407, 415; Mulvaney, 1990: 101); many reggae songs use *Babylon* in their title (Mulvaney, 1990). See also *beast, brown-man government, colonial shitstem, Elizabitch, Four Great Pirates, Nebuchadnezzar, Pope, Whore of Babylon*

Babylonian Government   Dominican government (used in Dominica) [de Albuquerque, 1980: 238]

Babylonian name   a person's name before conversion to Rastafarianism; "Many of the brethren will simply say that their name is Rasta or Rastafari and will not give their 'Babylonian' name." (Owens, 1976: 10) Others take "Ras" (from the Amharic, meaning "head") as a title and retain only their given

---

[3]The original Wailers included Bob Marley, Peter Tosh, and Bunny Wailer.

name (e.g. "Ras Michael"). See also *raas*

backward reactionary (Chevannes, 1994: 168)

badness hooliganism, senseless violence (Davis and Simon, 1982: 69)

bag-o-wire betrayer (Davis and Simon, 1982: 69)

bald / baldhead / bald tail clean-shaven man (Cassidy and Le Page, 1980: 21; Pollard, 1985: 35), an intellectual (Barrett, 1988: 289), an undesirable (N.Y.C.P.D., 1985: 14), a non-Rastafarian (Chevannes, 1978: 249), a white. "Crazy Baldhead" is a Wailers song (White, 1989: 367, 428). *Baldhead* as pejorative may predate Rastafarian usage (see Major, 1994: 19). See *bathroom locks, beardsman, burn head, combsome, dreadlock, nubbies, rope head, three unclean spirits*

bandulu bandit; trickster (Davis and Simon, 1982: 69); from "bandit" + *ulu* (Jamaican Creole for "thief" [Cassidy and Le Page, 1980: 457])

bathroom locks long braids; dreadlocks that have been combed, shaved or stylized (Nicholas, 1979: 55). See also *bald, beardsman, dreadlock, nubbies, rope head, three unclean spirits*

beardsman a dreadlock who trims or shaves his hair (N.Y.C.P.D., 1985: 15). See also *bald, burn head, combsome, dreadlock, nubbies, rope head, three unclean spirits*

beast police (Faristzaddi, 1982); a synonym of *Babylon* (Chevannes, 1978: 255); a Biblical reference to the devil

billy goat an archaic, derogatory term for Rastafarians due to their alleged smell from lack of bathing (Chevannes, 1978: 132). Present day Rastafarians are generally frequent bathers. See also *goat, ram goat*

Blackheart Men   maledictum used against Rastafarians (Waters, 1985: 176; White, 1989: 26); lit. "blackhearted (i.e. evil) men." The Blackheart Man is a mythical figure in Jamaica, predating Rastafarianism. "The blackheart mon [man] lives in perpetual darkness... He carries night with him like a robe draped about his head... Flowing from it are tangled snake-finger locks, coiled about like the hissing, viperous mane of Medusa. The blackheart mon has no friends, no home, no family. A stranger to all, he lives in the 'gullies' (open drains) of the city and the lonely hollows of the country, enticing with candies and fair words all children who dare to stray from their mothers or who stay out alone past sundown. He takes them away, never to see their kin again. He consumes them, limb by limb, or presents them to Satan as slaves." (White, 1989: 70) Bunny Wailer, a Rastafarian reggae musician, recognized and accepted this accusation of Rastafarian as *Blackheart Man*. He turned it into a benedictum by producing an album called "Blackheart Man" (White, 1989: 281, 426, 428). One of Owens' (1976: 26) informants was named "Blackheart." See Clifton (1978: 151), *gorgon*

blind   1. sinful; a non-Rastafarian (Faristzaddi, 1982) 2. cigarette (Yawney, 1979a: 220). See also *lowarette*

*Blind-aga   Edward Seaga, the head of the Jamaica Labour Party (J.L.P.) and former Prime Minister. This word is not Rasta Talk, but was co-opted by the rival People's National Party (P.N.P.) [Waters, 1985: 179]. *Blind-aga* is in Pollard's Category II, since the "see" sound of Seaga is changed to "blind." Word play on the Prime Minister's name is a popular pastime among all Jamaicans, so it is not clear how much Rastafarians contribute to such terms as *Blind-aga* and *C.I.A.-ga.* E.g., *SEAGA* ("Sell Everything and Go Abroad.") and *I.M.F.* ("It's Manley's Fault.") [I.M.F. is the abbreviation for the International Monetary Fund] are not attributed to Rastafarians (Meyer, 1985). See also *bustamente, men-lie, men-low*

blindjaret tobacco cigarette. From *blind* + "cigarette." The "see" sound in "cigarette" is converted to "blind" (Pollard, 1985: 36). Some Rastafarians shun tobacco cigarettes as a product of *Babylon*. Other Rastafarians use tobacco and refer to it as *frunto* ("turned from 'back' [i.e. 'bacco] to 'frunto'" [Faristzaddi, 1982]). There may be a distinction made by Rastafarians between commercial (i.e., *Babylonian*) tobacco and homegrown *frunto*. See also *lowarette*

blindza money (used in Barbados). From *blind* + *dunza* (Pollard, 1984: 60)

Blood! / Blood bath! An expression of disapproval (Chevannes, 1978: 183, 192, 253). See also *Blood clot!, Fire!*

Blood-and-fire Rastafari! a pseudonym adopted by a Rastafarian in a court of law (Chevannes, 1978: 184). See also *Blood!, Fire!, Rastafari*

Blood clot! 1. "heathen, the term of opprobrium derived from both menstruation, and the cloth with which slaves cleansed themselves after vicious beatings" (White, 1989: 26, 335); bad, equated with "cocksucker" (N.Y.C.P.D., 1985: 14) 2. menstrual pad (Luntta, 1991: 44). There is confusion about whether the word is "cloth" or "clot": in Jamaican Creole, /θ/ has converged phonologically with /t/ (Cassidy and Le Page, 1980: lviii). This and the other *clot/cloth* epithets that follow are either Jamaican Creole or directly derivable from Jamaican Creole, but they are probably used more frequently by Rastafarians than by other

Jamaicans, due to Rastafarian prohibitions for menstruating women. Similarly, the words may be more powerful for Rastafarians than for other Jamaicans. Davis and Simon (1992: 75) rank *blood clot, ras clot, bumbo clot,* and *pussy clot* as progressively more obscene terms in the "Rasta system of curses." The N.Y.C.P.D. (1985: 14) also rank these curses, not inconsistently with Davis and Simon, but academic researchers have not ranked them. Notably, *"Blood!"* is not listed in either ranking though it is a minor oath. Sobo (1993: 59) reports that menstrual blood itself is not considered unclean among Jamaicans, but it is the clotting within the blood, which is unclean.

Bobo a Rastafarian sect (Chevannes, 1978: 195-217; 1994: 171-188). In Jamaican Creole, *bobo* means both "fool" and "pretty" (Cassidy and Le Page, 1980: 57)

*bombo See *bumbo*

*bongo   See *bungo*

brown-man governments   Jamaican governments (Nettleford, 1970: 30, 61, 125). Due to British colonial influence, Jamaica has been ruled primarily by light-skinned people. A tripartite view of race relations is common in Jamaica: the white, British colonialists; the brown, minority mixed races and Asians who largely replaced the colonialists; and the disenfranchised black majority. See also *Babylon*

bulled king   King George VI who according to the Rastafarians, was "proclaimed but not crowned King" and who therefore "had no authority and could command no allegiance from his so-called subjects." (Chevannes, 1978: 151-152) To the Rastafarians of the time, Haile Selassie was the antithesis of George VI. That he was called a *bulled king* probably referred to the Jamaican Creole word *bull-bucker*, "a bully" or "someone who is assuming power over others." (Cassidy and Le Page,

31

1980: 77; Partridge, 1984: 152).
See also *Elizabitch, Nebuchadnez-zar*

*bumba / bumbo Cunt, arse. This word is Jamaican Creole; its use in Jamaican courts may result in a fine (Levine, 1980: 20)[4]

*Bumbo clot! Cunt clot! Arse clot! (Cassidy and Le Page 1980: 79); equated with "motherfucker" by the N.Y.C.P.D. (1985: 14). The late Peter Tosh, a Rastafarian and reggae musician, recorded songs called "Oh Bumbo Klaat" and "Bombo Klaat" (White, 1989: 339, 421, 423; Campbell, 1992). Tosh was widely regarded to have a sharp tongue (Sheridan, 1987: 22, 24), and was sometimes known as the "Stepping Razor", also one of the Wailers songs (White, 1989: 409, 412, 422;

---

[4]Similarly in English, two other words have existed in perineal limbo: "fanny" and "prat", both meaning either "cunt" or "arse", depending on the time and place of use.

Tafari, 1988: 18; Campbell, 1992). See also *blood clot, bungo clot, raas clot*

bumbo-cratic society sex-obsessed society (Yawney, 1976: 262). See also *pussycratic*

*****Bumbo raas clot!** Arse cloth! This is attributed to Peter Tosh (Ama, 1988b: 19), but *Bungo raas clot!* ("black arse cloth"), a near-homonym, would have made more sense since *bumbo* and *raas* are effectively synonyms.

*****bungo** Jamaican Creole for someone who is "very black, ugly, stupid, a country bumpkin, African, etc." (Cassidy and Le Page, 1980: 80; Cassidy 1982: 158). de Albuquerque (1979: 44) equates *bungo* with *nigger*, however *nigger* is also used in Jamaican Creole the same as in English. *Bungo* has been given benediction by the Rastafarians as evidenced by some taking it as part of their name, e.g., "Bongo (black) Lenny" (Nicholas, 1979: 39-40) and by the use of

Bungonyiah (*Bungo* + *niyabingi*)
[Pollard, 1982: 35]. Other religious minorities in Jamaica have
also been known as *Bungos* (e.g.
see Hogg, 1960: 3-4).

*Bungo clot! Stupid clot! Nigger clot![5]
See also *blood clot, bumbo clot,
raas cloth*

*bungo man See *bungo*

**Bungo nostrilise: dis country 'Im seet
and vomit thru Him eyes** Breathe
this in black brother: "God will
see what is going on and punish
people" (the curse of the Bobos)
[Dance, 1985: 91]. This is an example of Rastafarians turning a
maledictum (*bungo*) into a benedictum within the context of a
curse! See *bobo*

buried food canned food (Nicholas
1979: 58). See also *Arnold,*

---

[5]A similar phrase exists in United States
English, but not as an exclamation: see
negro cloth and *negro cotton* in
Eisiminger (1979: 167).

34

duppy, lotal, morgue, saalting, that thing

Burn! / Burn them! (Chevannes, 1978: 180, 253). See *Fire!*

burn head Rastafarian who shaves (Edward, n.d.: 14). Burn in Jamaican Creole can mean "to rub off the skin by sudden abrasion" (Cassidy and Le Page, 1980: 82). See also *bald, bathroom locks, beardsman, combsome, dreadlock, nubbies, rope head, three unclean spirits*

Burn the wicked! epithet used when smoking ganja (Yawney, 1979b: 168). See also *dread, Fire!*

Bustamente Alexander Bustamante, founder of the J.L.P. and former Prime Minister (Chevannes, 1978: 192). See also *Blind-aga, C.I.A.-ga, men, men-lie, men-low*

buy-I East Indians (corruption of *Niyabingi*, referring to the fact that many East Indians in Jamaica as merchants) [Yawney, 1979b: 251]

Caesar money (Faristzaddi, 1982; Edward, n.d.: 28; Owens, 1976: 73); a Biblical reference

Caesar system (Owens, 1976: 72). See *Babylon*

careless Ethiopian a person of African ancestry who is a non-Rastafarian (Chevannes, 1978: 267; Edward n.d.: 44). Rastafarians often equate Africa with Ethiopia

cemetery the body of someone who has been sterilized (Johnson-Hill, 1988: 391)

chuckee bad (de Albuquerque, 1980: 244)

Chris Thievin' Cumbolus Christopher Columbus (Peter Tosh in Aylmer, 1992: 20). See *pirate*

*C.I.A.-ga Edward Seaga. Waters (1985: 174) cites the usage of this term from a non-Rastafarian, however Seaga has often been disliked by Rastafarians. Waters (1985: 174-175) and White (1989: 304-334) give examples of Rastafarian sentiment against the United States Central Intelligence Agency prior to the time of the citation. Other anti-Seaga terms, not necessarily Rastafarian in origin, include *spyaga* ("spy" + "Seaga") and *liarga* ("liar" + "Seaga") [Davis and Simon, 1982: 51]. See also *Blind-aga, Bustamente, men-lie, men-low, Pharaoh Government*

clapping beef having sex with a woman (de Albuquerque, 1980: 244). *Beef* is English slang for "human flesh" and to *"be in a woman's beef* [formerly meant] to coït with her" (Partridge, 1984: 64). Clap means to "hit, break [or] strike" (Davis and Simon, 1982: 69). *Beef* is English slang for the female labia (Green, 1986: 33) or for human flesh (Partridge, 1984: 64). It is common, particularly among patriarchal groups such as the Rastafari, for men to analogize women with animals, and sex with hunting (Kitzinger, 1969: 259; Mills, 1989: xviii-xix;

Fiddes, 1991: 144-162). See also
skeef, welding

colonial shitstem Jamaican government
(Peter Tosh in Waters, 1985: 232).
From "shit" + "system." See also
Babylon, shitstem

combsome / comb head Rastafarian
without dreadlocks, and who is
thus able to comb his/her hair.
Nearly all Rastafarians today have
dreadlocks, but the early Rastafarians (prior to 1960) were mostly
combsome (Chevannes, 1978: 158;
Edward, n.d.: 14). Rastafarians first
wore *dreadlocks* in the late 1940s
(Chevannes, 1978: 171). See also
*bald, bathroom locks, beardsman,
burn head, nubbies, rope head,
three unclean spirits*

commercial dreadlocks *dreadlocks*
worn by a non-Rastafarian, a non-
Rastafarian who has *dreadlocks*

Concrete Jungle a slum in Kingston; a
song by the Wailers (White, 1989:
409); not necessarily Rastafarian
in origin. See *Dungle*

Condemned things! You have done something condemned! (Nicholas, 1979: 3)

curseblind oil kerosene oil (Yawney, 1979b: 172)

damagers [music industry] managers (Peter Tosh in Aylmer, 1992: 21)

deaders / dedaz / dedders meat; most Rastafarians are primarily vegetarian except for eating of small fish. From *dead + arse*

Devil the white world (Kitzinger, 1969: 250, 256, 258), a white man (Yawney, 1979a: 356; Simpson, 1980: 223)

Devil in disguise Christian preacher (Peter Tosh in Waters, 1985: 48)[6]

---

[6]Elijah Muhammad and Malcolm X used the terms "devils" or "blue-eyed devils" to refer to whites (Johnson, 1972: 142; Haley and X, 1965). The Christian church in Jamaica had been exclusively Eurocentric until the establishment of the Ethiopian Coptic Church in 1969 (not to be confused

dirty John Crow an archaic, derogatory name for Rastafarians (Chevannes, 1978: 277). In Jamaican Creole, *John Crow* is a buzzard, a scavenger, and a proverbial figure with "unfavorable traits attributed to the negro." *John Crow* may have the same origins as the United States English "Jim Crow." (Cassidy and Le Page, 1980: 250). See also *John Crow*

down-gress to denigrate (Nicholas, 1979: 46). From "down" + "progress"

downpressor oppressor; "The knowledge of Rastafari puts an end to this confusion of Babylon, used to fool the people of the world by giving the oppressor his true and rightful name, by changing the 'up' sound of 'op' to 'down.' A *downpressor* is literally one who presses one down to the ground in downpression." (Faristzaddi, 1982) The Wailers recorded the songs

with the Ethiopian Zion Coptic Church).

"Downpressor" and "Downpressor Man" (White, 1989: 401-402, 409).

downstroy destroy; from "down" + "destroy"

dread 1. strict (Barrett, 1988: 138); serious; dangerous (Davis and Simon, 1982: 69) 2. epithet used when smoking ganja (Yawney, 1979b: 168) 3. *dreadlock* 4. a Rastafarian in Dominica (de Albuquerque, 1980: 283; Meditz and Hanratty, 1989: 284), a Rastafarian 5. a Rastafarian impostor (Luntta, 1991: 51) 6. used as a maledictum against Rastafarians ("those dreadful people") [Simpson, 1980: 219]. See also *Burn the wicked!, fashionist, Fire!, fox, goat, jackass, wolf*

dreadlock long, matted hair; someone with long, matted hair; a Rastafarian. "To the elite it refers to an unkempt, dangerous, and dirty appearance." (Barrett 1988: 138). The wearing of *dreadlocks* is illegal in the British Virgin Islands

(Lorde, 1990: 40, 110), is effectively illegal in Antigua (Ama 1988a: 32), and was illegal in Dominica (de Albuquerque, 1980: 238; Meditz and Hanratty, 1989: 284). The difference between a *dreadlock* and a *Rastafarian* is not always clear, particularly among non-Rastafarians. *Dreadlocks* are the most obvious symbol of Rastafarianism, but a person with *dreadlocks* is not necessarily a Rastafarian. In Dominica, this difference has been muddled by Rastafarians calling themselves *Dreads*. In Antigua, immigration officials have been instructed to exclude Rastafarians, presumably by incorrectly identifying anyone with *dreadlocks* as a Rastafarian (Ama, 1988a: 32). In 1974, the Dominican government enacted "the so-called Dread Act [which] forbade criminal or civil proceedings against any person who killed or injured a member of an unlawful society or association [including Rastafarians]." (Meditz and Hanratty, 1989: 284) The Dread Act has since been repealed (de Albuquerque, 1980: 238). See also *bald, bathroom locks, beardsman, burn head, combsome, commercial dreadlocks, nubbies, rope head, three unclean spirits*

*Dungle one of the poorest slum area of Kingston; from "dung hill" + "jungle" (Dance, 1985: 207-208). "The inhabitants of the Dungle were not spoken of by anyone, their very existence acknowledged only by an assiduous avoidance of the precinct." (White, 1989: 113). Many early Rastafarians originated from the *Dungle*, but though the word coinage is Rastafarian in style (Pollard's Category II), it has not been definitively attributed to them. *Dungle* was originally called "Downhill" (Chevannes, 1978: 167) or "Dung Hill" (Clarke, 1975: 79). The Dungle was initially a raw sewage depository on the seacoast of Kingston (Patterson, 1964: 23), hence it was both downhill from Kingston and a dunghill of Kingston; it later became a garbage dump and squatter settlement. The English words "dung" and "down" have phonologically converged to /dong/ in Jamaican Creole, hence the origin will probably remain obscure (Cassidy and Le Page, 1980: 156; 164). See also *concrete jungle, John Crow*

duns / dunsa / dunza / dunzai money, "the filthy lucre of Babylon, used to continually buy and sell the creation of God thus keeping man in slavery to all that glitters which is not gold." (Faristzaddi, 1982) *Dunza* is derived from "done" (money is something that is always done, i.e. never around) according to Pollard (1984: 60) but it is possibly from "to dun."

duppy meat (used in Barbados) [Pollard, 1984: 61]; A duppy is a ghost in Jamaican Creole and in Barbados Creole. "Unlike the rather drab, colorless ghosts that float around in European lore, Jamaican duppies take on many interesting and different forms and personalities.... Duppies are sometimes playful, sometimes helpful, and sometimes cruel and vengeful, but since one never knows whether the duppy is a good or a bad one, the sight of a duppy usually inspires fear." (Dance, 1985: 35-36) Though *duppy*, the ghost, is not a maledictum, this original meaning imparts a negative connotation to meat eating: eating something that is a spirit with human characteristics (i.e. equating carnivorism with cannibalism). See also *Arnold, buried food, lotal, morgue, saalting, that thing*

dutty tils archaic maledictum used against Rastafarians (Waters, 1985: 176); lit. "shit-arses." From "dirty tails" (Cassidy and Le Page, 1980: 166)

Elizabitch "H.R.H. Queen Elizabeth of England; the 'symbolic' downpressor of the Black man and non-white peoples. The head representative of the Babylonian Harlot power ruling over all downpressed peoples." (Faristzaddi, 1982)

45

Elizabitch would probably apply to both Elizabeth I and II, since the latter is considered the reincarnation of the former (Davis and Simon, 1992: 73; Owens, 1976: 76). A Rastafarian named "Elizabeth" would be called *Izabeth.* See also *Babylon, bulled king, Nebuchadnezzar, Whore of Babylon*

fashionist someone who looks like a Rastafarian to be stylish but who does not have Rastafarian beliefs. See also *fox, goat, jackass, wolf*

Fire! / Fiyah! 1. "Rastafari greeting calling upon the cosmic fire to purify the creation. Can be used, and is used by Rastafarians to scold wrongdoers warning them that the cosmic fire will consume them if they do not perform the right works as a person grounded in righteousness should." (Faristzaddi 1982); a declaration of hostility (Chevannes, 1978: 180) 2. epithet used when smoking ganja (Yawney, 1979b: 168) 3. a signal that police are coming (N.Y.C.P.D.,

1985: 14). Probably alludes to the Bible as well as to smoking ganja. See also *Blood!, Burn the wicked, dread*

fleshy 1. a carnal person (maledictive) 2. a relative (benedictive) [Farist-zaddi, 1982]. Some Rastafarians have believed that a Rastafarian would not die unless he became sinful

follytricks politics; from "folly" + "tricks" (Hurford and Moore, n.d.: 24). See also *politickians*

Four Great Pirates 1. John Hawkins, Cecil Rhodes, "Stanley Livingstone" [Henry Morton Stanley and David Livingstone], and Ulysses S. Grant (Davis and Simon, 1992: 73) 2. Hawkins, Rhodes, Livingstone, and Grant (Smith *et al.*, 1978: 19). See also *Babylon, Elizabitch, Four Great Pirates, Nebuchadnezzar, pirate, Pope*

fox Rastafarian poseur who is a trickster (Tafari, 1985: 4).   See also *fashionist, goat, jackass, wolf*

fuckery "The Rastafarians teach that the proper use of herbs [ganja] has a central role to play in freeing the mind from the fuckery of colonialism." (Yawney, 1979b: 169) "You should not say that Jamaica is full of happy folks or fookery [sic] like that." (Bongo Sylly quoted in Davis and Simon [1992: 60]).   Possibly from "fuck" + "trickery"

germs Germans; America (Pollard, 1976: 249)

goat Rastafarian poseur who is a hypocrite (Tafari, 1985: 4).   See also *billy goat, fashionist, fox, jackass, ram goat, wolf*

gorgon 1. "king, bully, a person who is tops in what he does; toughest; best; ruthless person" (Pollard, 1982: 31) 2. the name of a Rastafarian (Chevannes, 1978: 173) 3. "outstanding dreadlocks" (Davis and Simon, 1982: 69). Gorgon, the snake-haired Greek mythical figure, is alluded to by *dreadlocks*. See also *blackeart men*

go up on it smoke ganja (a sexual allusion for a sacred act) [Yawney, 1979b: 167]. The sacred and profane are intimately and historically linked. Arango (1989: 41, 45-47, 82-87), for instance, details that submission to God is often a symbolic sexual submission. See also *rape the chalice*

"grimy tattered followers of the Lion of Judah" Rastafarians, as referred to by Maingot (1980: 48). The Lion of Judah is a symbol of Rastafarians

head-decay-shun education (Bob Marley in Cooper, 1995: 121)

heil Hail "is a Rastafarian greeting taken from the first name of the Emperor, Haile" Selassie (Faristzaddi, 1982). *Heile* is "strength" or "power" in Amharic (Kane, 1990: 25). Waters (1985: 129) states that the P.N.P. co-opted "hail" from the Rastafarians, but the J.L.P. countered by associating the phrase with *Heil Hitler!*

Hell Jamaica (Yawney, 1979a: 356; Simpson, 1980: 222; Barrett, 1988, 104)

Hellfire and brimstone! (Biblical reference). See also *Fire!*

Hellfire and damnation! (Biblical reference) [Nicholas, 1979: 3]. See also *Fire!*

hot stepper fugitive (Davis and Simon, 1982: 69)

isms and schisms the result of the *shitstem*'s policy of divide and conquer (Davis and Simon, 1982: 69). Note that a similar phrase was used in 1680: "He was the great Hieroglyph of Jesuitism, Puritanism, Quaquerism [sic], and of all the Isms of Schism." ('Heraclio Democritus' [1680]. *Vision of Purgatory*. p. 46, cited in Hughes, 1991: 126) The use of -ism and -ist as pejorative sectarian suffixes dates to the 1500s (Hughes, 1991: 93-94, 130). See *Pope*

Iyabingi the Rastafarian way of life, a Rastafarian spiritual gathering, a drumming style on which reggae is based. "The popular interpretation of Niyabinghi/ Iyabinghi is 'Death to the Black and White *downpressors*'" (Faristzaddi, 1982; Smith *et al.*, 1978: 7-8). The word *Niyabingi* comes from the name of a central African anti-colonialist religion. It originally meant, "one who possesses greatness." (Pauwels, 1951: 22)

jackass Rastafarian poseur (Tafari, 1985: 4). See also *fox, goat, wolf*

Jamdown / Jamdung Jamaica; "a place that jams... [ellipsis his] or keeps one down" (Faristzaddi 1982); As noted earlier, many Rastafarians now have had a more positive view of Jamaica. Benedicta for Jamaica are: *Jahmekya* ("*Jah makes here*"), *Jah-maker*, *Jamakka* (*Jah* + *makka*; *makka* is a kind of ganja [Faristzaddi,

1982]), and *J.A.* These all allude to *Jah*, another name that Rastafarians use for Selassie. *Jah* is etymologically derived from "Yahweh" (i.e. Jehovah). To *jam* means to *downpress*, as in this case, to dance, to fuck (Waters, 1985: 264), or to make music. The latter three meanings are also used in British and American slang (e.g. see Paros, 1984: 25)

jead defiantly ragged; probably from *jege* (Jamaican Creole: "torn" or "tattered")+ *dread* (Cassidy and Le Page, 1980: 244; Johnson-Hill, 1988: 267-268)

jester / jestering "kidding; joking, playing around; not sincere, not acting right" (Pollard, 1982: 31)

Jesus / Jeezsus 1. Jesus 2. money (Owens, 1976: 106); "Rastafari know the pronunciation of Jeezsus is given by Babylon conjures evil vibrations so that when the people pray and think they are praying to God they are really praying to the devil." (Faristzaddi, 1982) "Jesus",

as pronounced in standard English
(/jēzes/), is considered an evil figure, but pronounced as /jesus/, is
considered the true messiah
(Owens, 1976: 106-107). This
phonological dichotomy is not
universal among Rastafarians. See
also *pie-in-the-sky-when-you-die,
religion*

Jesus government (Owens, 1976: 82);
see also *Babylon*

jinalship trickery (Owens, 1976: 201); a
jinal is a clever person or crook in
Jamaican Creole (Cassidy and Le
Page, 1980: 247)

John Crow a non-Rastafarian inhabi-
tant of the *Dungle* who ate condemned food (Kitzinger, 1971:
583). "[Peter] Tosh denounced all
singing toasters like Yellowman,
as well as the newer dance-hall
DJs calling them 'district John-
Crows.'" (White, 1989: 356)
"Toasting" and "dance-hall" are
reggae music styles that are often
lacking in Rastafarian ideology, so
John Crow may be a more general

maledictum against non-Rastafarians (Sheridan, 1987: 28). See also *dirty John Crow*

Ku Klux society racist society (Owens, 1976: 246)

Lightning! (Chevannes, 1978: 280). See *Fire!*

locksman See *dreadlock*

lotal religiously unclean food, e.g. pork (used in Barbados) [Pollard, 1984: 60]. *Ital* is clean, wholesome food; Rastafarian reggae. From *low + Ital*. Cassidy and Le Page (1980: 498) have suggested that *Ital = I +* "vital", Jacobs (1985: 122) claims it is from *I +* "total", Yawney (1979a: 136) claims it is from *I +* "natural", and I have even heard *Ital = I +* "vittle." In Rasta Talk, *I* is synonymous and homophonic with the standard English "high" (and "I" and "eye"), hence the formation of the antonym *lotal* from *Ital*. See also *Arnold, buried food, duppy, morgue, saalting, that thing*

lowarette cigarette (Yawney, 1979a: 220); from "low" + "cigarette"; see also *blind, blindjaret*

Lucifer World (Edward, n.d.: 35) See *Pharaoh World*

madvisors [financial] advisors (Peter Tosh in Aylmer, 1992: 21). From "mad" + "advisors"

mad weed immature ganja that is full of seeds, and hence of low potency (Yawney, 1979a: 178)

me See *men*

megry "business turned sour" (Pollard, 1982: 31). Possibly derived from: *mek-mek* which is "quarreling" in Jamaican Creole (Cassidy and Le Page, 1980: 298), or from *meg* which was British slang for "to swindle" (Partridge, 1984: 731).

men "evil or wicked person" (Farist-zaddi, 1982), inauthentic person (Owens, 1976: 67); a homosexual (Pollard, 1985: 39; Pollard, 1990). Rastafarians use *I, I-man, I-n-I,* or *man* to replace *men* for benedic-

55

tion. The reason the word *men* is denigrated is because of the Rastafarians' worship of a holy singularity: man is God, and all men are one (Owens, 1976: 65-66). Consequently, Rastafarians have also replaced all pronouns with I-forms (Pollard's Category III.i.) or with *man*: other pronouns are considered derogatory. Black Americans have used the phrase "the man" to refer to whites or the police as an expression of black emasculation (Johnson, 1972: 142-143; Clifton, 1978: 162). Emasculation is also a reason for Rastafarians making *men* a maledictum. The use of the I–words that replace *men* is a Rastafarian rejection of the Jamaican Creole use of *me* in place of *I*, an indication of self-deference towards colonialists (Owens, 1976: 65).[7] Homosexuality is considered

---

[7]This pronominal replacement (Waters, 1985: 106) is akin to the Quakers' use of the archaic form of the third person singular, "thou" (Fox *et al.*, 1968: 3; Hughes, 1991: 98) and the pronominal substitution used in a Papua New

Guinea cargo cult (Schwartz, 1962: 327). All three of these instances of pronominal substitution reflect the desire to make language congruent with religion, a desire noted in Fell (1989: 14). Also reflected in the substitution is reaction against colonialism, in the case of Rastafarians and cargo cultists; and against aristocracy, in the case of Quakers. Kitzinger (1971: 587) notes other parallels between Rastafarians and early Quakers: both arose "from the very rabble and dregs of the people" and both "often used highly abusive language." But in contrast to Rastafarians, the early Quakers did not swear (Hughes, 1991: 164-165), at least not as far as has been documented.

Another parallel between the Rastafarians and some Cargo Cults is the development of a secret language register (Schwartz, 1962; Mühlhäusler, 1979: 339-342).

The formation of a millennial religion is a common reaction to colonization (Thrupp, 1970) and more generally to defeat (La Barre, 1970), but the formation of secret language registers in connection with millenialism appears to evil by Rastafarians because of their interpretation of the Bible. See *unu*

men language Standard Jamaican English, i.e. standard English as spoken in Jamaica, the language of the Jamaican elite (Johnson-Hill, 1988: 297-298)

Men-lie / Men-low Michael Manley, head of the P.N.P. (Chevannes, 1978: 192). See also *Blind-aga, Bustamente, C.I.A.-ga*

morgue refrigerator (Pollard, 1982: 31). Food that is not fresh is not considered *Ital.* See also *Arnold, buried food, duppy, lotal, saalting, that thing*

---

be limited to Rastafarians and to a limited number of Melanesian Cargo Cults. This secrecy could actually be more widespread (but undocumented), since the colonizers against whom the secrets are kept are usually the documenters.

nappie nappy (fuzzy). This word is a Jamaican Creole (and English) malediction for naturally fuzzy hair that has not been straightened. It has been applied to Rastafarians with *dreadlocks*. There may be some phonological confusion with *nattie*. For example, Campbell (1987: 95) states, "Parents would sometimes curse their children as '*nattie head pickney* [natty headed pickaninny].'" and Pollard (1982: 31) equates *natty* with unkempt or kinky hair. Cassidy and Le Page state that some English /p/ sounds have become /t/ in Jamaican Creole (1980: lviii), but they do not otherwise indicate that Jamaican Creole has different meanings for *nattie* or *nappie* than standard English. Rastafarians, however, often refer to their hair as *nattie* ("natty") *dreadlocks*, and so may have been a benedictive pun on *nappie*

Nebuchadnezzar Edward VIII is considered to be the reincarnation of this Babylonian King (Davis and

59

Simon, 1992: 73; Smith *et al.*, 1978: 19). See also *Babylon, bulled king, Elizabitch*

Niyabingi See *Iyabingi*

nubbies *dreadlocks* in their first stage of growth (de Albuquerque, 1980: 244). See also *bald, bathroom locks, beardsman, rope head, three unclean spirits*

ombre to be aggressive, an aggressor (used in Barbados). "There was a man called 'Ombray' (hombre?), an aggressive type of fellow who functioned on the periphery of a group of Rastas whenever he was out of trouble/jail. His name has been applied to predatory and aggressive behaviour of the type associated with him." (Pollard, 1984: 61). The word *hombre* in American English slang however has had a similar connotation (a bad or tough man), but with a clear Spanish origin (Adams, 1968: 151). See also *wolf*

outformer   police informer (Pollard, 1982: 33); from "out" + "informer"

outiquity   "A person of 'iniquity'" (Faristzaddi 1982); from "out" + "iniquity"

outvention "Man's insatiable appetite, creating more inventions for his ever changing material existence." (Faristzaddi, 1982) From "out" + "invention"; see also *tricknology*

paku-blind   white person (Yawney, 1976: 261); from *patu* (Jamaican Creole: "ugly person", *patu-eye* = "albino negro" [Cassidy and Le Page, 1980: 342]) + *blind*

Pharaoh Government   J.L.P. (de Albuquerque, 1980: 245), a Biblical allusion.   See also *Babylon, Blind-Aga, C.I.A.-Ga*

Pharaoh world   neocolonialism. "…don't mix [these rights] with the national world (*X World*, European world and *Lucifer* and *Pharoah* [sic] *World*)" (Edward, n.d.: 35). These are the worlds of:

61

wrong, whites, evil, and neocolonialism, respectively

piaca American (Yawney, 1979a: 349a); refers to greediness; see *pyakism*

pie-in-the-sky-when-you-die Christianity. Rastafarians reject the Christian notion of afterlife rewards following earthly privation as a notion that is beneficial to colonialism and neocolonialism (Chevannes, 1978: 238-239; Owens, 1976: 85). Partridge (1984: 878) reports this phrase as being a "cynical American [catch phrase], implying that the hope of a happy hereafter is illusory." See also *Jesus, religion*

pirate a colonialist or neo-colonialist (Chevannes, 1978: 251, 253, 260). Peter Tosh gives Henry Morgan, Christopher Columbus and Francis Drake as examples (Campbell, 1992). See also *Chris Thievin' Cumbolus, Four Great Pirates*

political misleaders political leaders (Yawney, 1979a: 336)

politickians / politicks / polytricks / politricksians / polytricksters "Politics and politicians are full of tricks and are like ticks upon the backs of the people." (Faristzaddi, 1982). See also *follytricks*

pollution people who exist in spiritual darkness (Faristzaddi, 1982)

Pope 1. "The personifications and lineal representative of the devil, just as the Emperor [Selassie] is the personification of Jah [Jehovah] the Almighty... The Rastafari are pro-Christ, but anti-Christian as projected by the Pope, its head, a Christianity which does not upkeep the tenets laid by Christ." (Faristzaddi, 1982) 2. the head of the Mafia (Yawney, 1979b: 172). Ironically, "one million Irish schoolchildren assembled in Dublin in 1980 to sing their interpretation of the Melodians' 'Rivers of Babylon' to Pope John Paul II... The pontiff was unaware that the lovely 1970 rock-steady [a reggae precursor] ballad foretold the imminent demise of the religious principality he ruled."[8] (White, 1989: 332) "Kill Pope Paul and Babylon fall." is a Rastafarian chant (Grass, 1982: 62). Hughes (1991: 93-94) reports numerous maledicta relating to the papacy during The Reformation that were created via suffix, e.g. "papism" and "papist." Interestingly this form has not been recorded in Rasta Talk even though the suffix *-ism* is negatively valued. See also *Babylon, isms and schisms, Rome*

Pussy cloth! (Dance 1985: 79) See also *blood cloth, bumbo clot, bungo clot, raas cloth*

pussycratic sex-obsessed (Yawney, 1976: 261); from *pussy* + *democratic*. See also *bumbo-cratic society*

---

[8]The Melodians' song is an adaptation of a traditional Rastafarian lament (see Thelwell, 1980: 181).

64

pussycratzing fucking (Yawney, 1976: 260)

pyakism greed (de Albuquerque, 1980: 244). *Peaka-peow* in Jamaican Creole is a gambling game that was introduced by the Chinese (Cassidy and Le Page, 1980: 343). See also *piaca*

*raas Arse (Cassidy and Le Page, 1980: 372, 375); "Fuck [is] the nearest English equivalent." (Cashmore, 1979: 12). Dance (1985: 210) equates it with "arse" or "damn." Rastafarians have adopted the Amharic *ras* ("prince") even though it is a near homophone of one of the most vulgar words in Jamaican Creole, *raas* (Cassidy and Le Page, 1980: xlix-li, Kane, 1990: 381). It is unclear whether this is unintentional irony, or intentional inversion (e.g., see Owens, 1976: 110). Dance (1985: 77-78) gives two folk tales that utilize the confusion between *ras* and *raas*. Peter Tosh called Chris Blackwell, The Wailers' manager, "Ta fockin' raas wit' dis bullrush [bulla rush], pussy clot double-billin'!" (The fucking arse with this insulting, pussy-clot double-billing!) when he was disputing his lack of billing in the band (White 1989: 252). See also *Babylonian name, rude boy, Whiteworst*

raas Babylon someone without scruples (Yawney, 1979b: 165)

*Raas clot! / Ras clot! Arse (Cunt) cloth! (Dance, 1985: 79).

"... Because me born so rass-claat Black, me know sey me was a curse according to the shitstem dem time dey." (Because I was born so arse-cloth black, I know that I was a curse according to the shit-system of that time.) [Peter Tosh quoted in Ama 1988b: 19]. See also *bumbo clot, bungo clot, blood cloth, shitstem*

racketeer Christian revivalists (Simpson, 1980: 220)

ram goat 1. an archaic, derogatory term for Rastafarians due to their alleged smell from lack of bathing (Chevannes, 1978: 132) 2. a *beardsman* (Chevannes 1978: 174-175). See also *billy goat, goat*

rape the chalice smoke ganja (Yawney, 1979b: 167). See *go up on it*

ras-mance romance (Peter Tosh quoted in Cooper, 1995: 172); from *raas* + "romance"

*rass See *raas*

Rasta a Rastafarian. "Ten years ago, to call a stranger 'Rasta' in Jamaica was an insult, like calling him 'nigger.' Today, it is a compliment, an equivalent of 'comrade.'" (Mason, 1980: 139-140) See also *Rastafari*

Rasta clots Rastafarians (a police officer quoted in Davis and Simon, 1992: 78); from *Rastafarian* + *Raas clots*

Rastafari 1. Haile Selassie (Ras Tafari) 2. a Rastafarian. Owens (1976: 47) quoted a Rastafarian on the significance of the name, "We are of the base things of the earth, that Christ speak of in the Bible. We shall confound the wise and prudent and shall set up a new world through the power of His Majesty [Selassie]. For no one did know him but those who were called by his dreadful and terrible name, Rastafari." Similarly, White (1989: 45) wrote that Rastafari is "He Whose Name Should Not Be Spoken." See also *Rasta*

Rastaman-woman   a Rastafarian woman. Prior to 1975, "a 'Rastaman-woman' was a person who was told what to do, what to wear, and how to behave. Since 1975, the influx [from] the middle class of independent and intelligent women has changed the picture drastically. Today there are 'Rasta-women', not 'Rasta-men-women.'"   (Barrett, 1988: 242) See also *skeef*

reel and stagger like a drunkard   "is [a] heavy putdown" (Nicholas,

1979: 62).   Rastafarians prohibit alcohol consumption

religion   Christianity. "We don't business with religion! A colonial thing that! That is what the white man bring down here to enslave the black man!" (a Rastafarian quoted in Owens, 1976: 82) See also *Jesus, pie-in-the-sky-when-you-die, tricknological*

Rome   1. "the dwelling place of the devil and the symbol of degenerate Western civilization where Satan and his spirits carry out the prostitution of the world through the Vatican and the figurehead of the Pope" (Faristzaddi, 1982) 2. "the North American / European power complex" (Owens, 1976: 37); see also *Babylon, Pope*

Roman Soldiers of Babylon   probably a reference to the J.L.P. by the late Jacob Miller, a Rastafarian and reggae musician (Waters, 1985: 174-175, 183)

ropehead a Rastafarian with dreadlocks, used by a primarily white, *combsome* Rastafarian group known as the Ethiopian Zion Coptic Church (Barrett, 1988: 239). Campbell (1987: 115-118) calls the members of this church pseudo-Rastafarians. The benedictum is *dreadlock* or *locksman.* See also *bald, bathroom locks, beardsman, burn head, nubbies, three unclean spirits*

Rude Boy a violent criminal (Jamaican Creole) [Campbell, 1987: 112]; a violent, criminal Rastafarian poseur (N.Y.C.P.D., 1985: 39). Rude boys have sometimes been confused with Rastafarians. In addition to its English meaning, *rude* in Jamaican Creole means bold, wild, violent, reckless, sexually aggressive (Cassidy and Le Page, 1980: 387), and obscene (Dance, 1985: 54). See also *wolf*

Rudie See *rude boy*

saalting meat or fish; lit. "salt-thing" (Cassidy and Le Page, 1980: 388). Rastafarians disfavor meat, large fish, and salted food, so this word is a malediction. Saltiness also has a negative connotation among the general Jamaican population. It is associated with sweat and uncleanness (Sobo, 1993: 156-157). See also *arnold, buried food, duppy, lotal, morgue, that thing*

screw "to scowl, to be angry" (Davis and Simon, 1982: 69)

screwface 1. Satan (White, 1989: 237) 2. a tensed face (Tafari, 1988: 18). The Wailers recorded a song called "Screw Face" (White, 1989: 237, 408, 411, 435).

sexpool "Woman become the sexpool of corruption and man become the sexmaniac." (Ras Hu-I quoted in Nicholas, 1979: 65). Note: this is correct grammar, see *men*. Rastafarians prohibit sexual promiscuity, as well as birth control other than abstinence. From "sexpot" + "cesspool"

shitstem the system (Peter Tosh quoted in Wolynski *et al.*, 1978: 28; Tafari, 1988: 18; and Ama, 1988b: 25); from "shit" + "system"; see also *colonial shitstem*

shituation situation. Peter Tosh was quoted by Wolynski *et al.* (1978: 23) as decrying "'the colonialist imperialist shituation' of 'pirates who still come rob up the resources of the country,' the 'shitstem of class and color prejudice,' the oppressiveness of the legal system, and the ineffectuality of the political directorate [of Jamaica]" in front of "the island's leading politicians, the foreign press, and 25,000 wildly cheering Kingston youths." Shortly afterward, Tosh was arrested in a separate, but allegedly related incident in which he was charged with among other things, using indecent language (Wolynski *et al.*, 1978: 28; Campbell, 1992). From "shit" + "situation"; see also *tricknological*

skeef   girl, woman (Pollard 1982: 32). From "skin" + "beef" (in Jamaican Creole, *skin* can mean "body" [Cassidy and Le Page, 1980: 411]). A benedictum for "girl" or "young woman" is *virgin*, a benedictum for "woman" is *queen* (Kitzinger, 1969: 253). See also *clapping beef, rastaman-woman, welding*

sober mad   psychopathic (Yawney, 1979a: 157)

Sodom   1. birth control 2. Homosexuality (Kitzinger, 1969: 250)

Sodom and Gomorrah   Jamaican Government (Kitzinger, 1971: 581); a Biblical reference. See also *Babylon*

Sodomite   a Jamaican Government official (Chevannes, 1978: 182)

soft   "amateurish, unable to cope" (Davis and Simon, 1982: 69)

sufferation   from "suffer" + "situation" (de Albuquerque, 1980: 236; Edward, n.d.: 16)

that / that thing pork (Pollard, 1982: 30); see also *Arnold, duppy, lotal, morgue, saalting*

three unclean spirits combs, scissors, and razors (Nicholas, 1979: 46). Most Rastafarians interpret the Bible as prohibiting cutting or combing hair. See also *bald, bathroom locks, beardsman, burn head, combsome, dreadlock, nubbies, rope head*

tribal / tribalist troublesome (Pollard 1982: 32; Waters 1985: 149); reference to African tribal warfare

tricknological/tricknology "Our people have been divided for years under this shituational, religionistic, tricknological bullshit." (Peter Tosh in Boyle, 1987: 26; Aylmer, 1992: 20) From *trick + technological/technology*. See also *outvention, polytricks, religion, shituation*

U-blind the University of the West Indies (U.W.I.), the people at U.W.I. "The U.W.I. was formerly a

College of London University —
hence U.C.W.I. In the eyes of
Rasta they have not seen the truth
[Rastafarianism] so are **blind**."
(emphasis in original) [Pollard,
1985: 36] Rastafarians have taken
the "U.C." (pronounced "you
see") from "U.C.W.I." and turned
it into a malediction. See also
blind, men

undread 1. hundred 2. un-*dread* (i.e.
un-Rastafarian) [Johnson-Hill,
1988: 205]

unhola unholy (Faristzaddi, 1982). The
more common word, *hola*, is used
instead of holy because of perceived negative homophony with
"hole"

unu aliens, outsiders (Chevannes, 1978:
266). *Unu* is a Jamaican Creole
variant of "you" (usually plural,
and hence negatively valued in
Rasta Talk) [Cassidy and Le Page,
1980: 457]. See also *men*

vampire someone who kills for profit, someone who is part of *Babylon* (Johnson-Hill, 1988: 369)

vampire system see *Babylon*

vank shun (de Albuquerque, 1980: 244)

welding having sex (Davis and Simon, 1992: 30-31). In Jamaican Creole, sexual intercourse is referred to as "work" (Sobo, 1993: 173). See also *clapping beef, skeef*

white lie big lie (Kitzinger, 1969: 248)

white men a white, whites; the benedictum is "white man." See *men*

white wash de-Africanize (de Albuquerque, 1979: 44)

Whitewell, Chris Chris Blackwell, the manager of The Wailers (Peter Tosh in Sheridan, 1987: 26)

Whiteworst, Chris Chris Blackwell (Peter Tosh in White, 1989: 252)

Whore of Babylon Queens Elizabeth I and II (Sanders, 1982: 62). This term was also coined by Tyndale in 1530 as applied to the Pope as an allusion to the Bible (Revelation 17) [Hughes, 1991: 96]; it is likely that Rastafarians also took inspiration from this section of the Bible for creating this term. See also *Babylon, Elizabitch, Pope*

wolf Rastafarian poseur who is violent or deceitful (Tafari, 1985: 4); a member of the Ethiopian Zion Coptic Church (many Rastafarians believe that this church is more concerned with profiting from the sale of ganja than with the spiritual aspects of Rastafarianism) [Luntta, 1991: 52]. See also *fashionist, fox, goat, ombre, ropehead, rude boy*

woe-men, women woman, women. *Woman* means "woe to man" among Rastafarians who live independently from women (Yawney, 1979a: 120). The benedictum is *woman* or *I-woman*.

wooden suit coffin (Pollard, 1982: 33)[9]

X "X represent Satan kingdom, unjust kingdom, European Kingdom." (Edward n.d.: 44) This is probably a reinterpretation of "X" representing "Christ" (e.g. "Xmas"). Peter Tosh referred to himself as "Red X" because he always saw his name written next to one on official forms (Campbell, 1992), but this was possibly more echoic of Malcolm X who took his name in rejection of "the white slave-master name of 'Little' which some blue-eyed devil named Little had imposed upon [his] paternal forebears." (Haley and X, 1965: 199). See also *Jesus*

---

[9]*Wooden coat*, *wooden kimono*, and *wooden surtout* have been used with this meaning by the underworlds of Britain and the United States (Partridge, 1984: 1349; Partridge 1989[1950]: 777, 804). *The Oxford English Dictionary* (2nd ed.) lists *wooden kimono*, *wooden suit* and *wooden surtout* as slang for coffin. None of these phrases are reported in Cassidy and Le Page (1980).

X World the world of wrong, "the European world" (Edward, n.d.: 26, 35, 44). See also *Pharaoh World*

you See *men, unu*

You have crossed Selassie I! You have crossed with God! (Nicholas, 1979: 3)

zombie blind follower (Johnson-Hill, 1988: 213)

Zombie in a P.R.G. term of abuse used against the Rastafarians who fought in the Grenadian revolution and later joined the Provisional Revolutionary Government (Campbell, 1987: 165)[10]

---

[10]Partridge (1984: 1371) reports use of *zombie* as Canadian Army World War II slang for a conscript.

Bibliography

Adams, Ramon F. (1968). *Western Words: A Dictionary of the American West.* Norman: University of Oklahoma Press.

Ama, Imani Tafari (1988a). "Shock treatment for Rastafarians in Antigua." *Reggae Report* 6(1): 32.

Ama, Imani Tafari (1988b). "Peter Tosh speaks." *Reggae Report* 6(2): 19, 25.

Arango, Ariel C. (1989). *Dirty Words: Psychoanalytic Insights.* Northvale, NJ: Jason Aronson.

Aylmer, Kevin J. (1992). "In touch with Tosh." *Reggae Report* 10(8): 20-23.

Barrett, Leonard E. (1988). *The Rastafarians: Sounds of Cultural Dissonance.* Boston: Beacon Press.

Bishton, Derek (1986). *Black Heart Man: A Journey Into Rasta.* London: Chatto & Windus.

Bones, Jah (1986). "Language and Rastafari." In: *The Language of the Black Experience: Cultural Expression through Word and Sound in the Caribbean and*

Black Britain. David Sutcliffe and Ansel Wong, eds. New York: Basil Blackwell, pp. 37-51.

Boyle, Chris (1987). "Words, sound and power." *The Reggae & African Beat* 6(5): 24-26.

Campbell, Horace (1987). *Rasta and Resistance: From Marcus Garvey to Walter Rodney.* Trenton, New Jersey: Africa World Press.

Campbell, Nicholas, director (1992). *Stepping Razor — Red X (The Peter Tosh Story).* Great Britain: SC Entertainment International [film].

Cashmore, Ernest (1979). *Rastaman: The Rastafarian Movement in England.* Boston: George Allen & Unwin.

Cassidy, Frederic Gomes (1982). *Jamaica Talk: Three Hundred Years of the English Language in Jamaica.* London: Macmillan Education.

Cassidy, Frederic Gomes and Le Page, Robert Black (1980). *Dictionary of Jamaican English.* New York: Cambridge University Press.

Chevannes, Barry (1978). *Social Origins of the Rastafari Movement.*

Kingston, Jamaica: Institute of Social and Economic Research, University of the West Indies.

Chevannes, Barry (1994). *Rastafari: Roots and Ideology*. Syracuse: Syracuse University Press.

Clarke, Colin G. (1975). *Kingston, Jamaica: Urban Development and Social Change, 1692-1962*. Berkeley: University of California Press.

Clifton, Merritt (1978). "How to hate thy neighbor: A guide to racist maledicta." *Maledicta* 2: 149-174.

Cooper, Carolyn (1995). *Noise in the Blood: Orality, Gender, and the "Vulgar" Body of Jamaican Popular Culture*. Durham, NC: Duke University Press.

Dance, Daryl C. (1985). *Folklore from Contemporary Jamaicans*. Knoxville: University of Tennessee Press.

Darwin, Charles (1965 [1872]). *The Expression of the Emotions in Man and Animals*. Chicago: The University of Chicago Press.

Davis, Stephen and Simon, Peter, eds. (1982). *Reggae International*.

New York: Rogner & Bernhard GMBH.

Davis, Stephen and Simon, Peter, eds. (1992). *Reggae Bloodlines: In Search of the Music and Culture of Jamaica.* Garden City, New York: Da Capo Press, 2nd ed.

de Albuquerque, Klaus (1979). "The future of the Rastafarian movement." *Caribbean Review* 8(4): 22-25, 44-46.

de Albuquerque, Klaus (1980). "Rastafarianism and cultural identity in the Caribbean." *Revista/Review Interamericana* 10(2): 230-247.

Dillard, Joey Lee (1976). "Black names." In: *Contributions to the Sociology of Language*, Joshua A. Fishman, ed. No. 13. The Hague, Netherlands: Mouton.

Dundes, Alan (1980). *Interpreting Folklore.* Bloomington: Indiana University Press.

Dundes, Alan (1987). *Cracking Jokes: Studies of Sick Humor Cycles and Stereotypes.* Berkeley, CA: Ten Speed Press.

Edward, Prince Emmanuel Charles (n.d.) *Black Supremacy in Rightousness [sic] of Salvation Jesus Negus Christ Emmanuel "I" Selassie "I" Jah Rastafari in Royal Majesty Selassie "I" Jahovah Jah Rastafar "I."* Jamaica: Jerusalem School Room of the Ethiopia Africa International Congress.

Eisiminger, Sterling (1979). "A glossary of ethnic slurs in American English." *Maledicta* 3(2): 153-174.

Faristzaddi, Millard (1982). *Itations of Jamaica and I Rastafari ...the First Itation.* New York: Grove Press. [no pagination]

Fell, G. S. (1989). "Explorations into linguistic practice as a source of religious polarities, or the inevitability of ineffability." In: *Language in Religion,* Humphrey Tonkin and Allison Armstrong Keef, eds. New York: University Press of America, pp. 7–15.

Fiddes, Nick (1991). *Meat: A Natural Symbol.* New York: Routledge.

Fox, George, Stubs, John, and Furly, Benjamin (1968 [1660]). *A Battle–Door for Teachers & Professors to Learn Singular and Plural*. Menston, England: The Scolar Press. [pagination irregular]

Grass, Randall (1982). "Do the reggay." In: Davis and Simon, pp. 45-47.

Green, Jonathon (1986). *The Slang Thesaurus*. New York: Viking Penguin.

Haley, Alex and X, Malcolm (1965). *The Autobiography of Malcolm X*. New York: Ballantine Books.

Hogg, Donald (1960). "The Convince Cult in Jamaica." *Yale University Publications in Anthropology* 58.

Hughes, Geoffrey (1991). *Swearing: A Social History of Foul Language, Oaths and Profanity in English*. Cambridge, MA: Basil Blackwell.

Hurford, Ray and Moore, Colin (n.d.). "Willie Williams — songs of consolation." *Small Axe* 20: 22-25.

Jacobs, Virginia Lee (1985). Roots of Rastafari. San Diego, CA: Slawson Communications.

Johnson, Ken (1972). "The vocabulary of race." In: *Rappin' and Stylin' Out: Communication in Urban*

Black America, Thomas Kochman, ed. Chicago: University of Illinois Press, pp. 140-151.

Johnson-Hill, Jack Anthony (1988). *Elements of an Afro-Caribbean Social Ethic: A Disclosure of the World of Rastafari as Liminal Process*. Ph.D. Thesis: Vanderbilt University.

Jones, Simon (1988). *Black Culture, White Youth: The Reggae Tradition from JA to UK*. London: Macmillan Education.

Kane, Thomas Leiper (1990). *Amharic-English Dictionary*. Wiesbaden, Germany: Otto Harrassowitz.

Kitzinger, Sheila (1969). "Protest and mysticism: The Rastafari Cult of Jamaica." *Journal for the Scientific Study of Religion* 8: 240-262.

Kitzinger, Sheila (1971). "The Rastafarian brethren of Jamaica." In: *Peoples and Cultures of the Caribbean: An Anthropological Reader,* Michael M. Horowitz, ed. Garden City, New York: Natural History Press, pp. 580-588.

La Barre, Weston (1970). *The Ghost Dance: The Origins of Religion*. Garden City, NY: Doubleday.

Legman, Gershon (1964). *The Horn Book: Studies in Erotic Folklore and Bibliography*. New Hyde Park, NY: University Books.

Legman, Gershon (1975). *Rationale of the Dirty Joke: An Analysis of Sexual Humor*. Second Series. New York: Breaking Point.

Levine, Robert M. (1980). *Race and Ethnic Relations in Latin America and the Caribbean: An Historical Dictionary and Bibliography*. Metuchen, New Jersey: Scarecrow Press.

Littlewood, Roland (1993). *Pathology and Identity: The Word of Mother Earth in Trinidad*. New York: Cambridge University Press.

Lourde, Audre (1990). "Is your hair still political?" *Essence* 21(5): 40, 110.

Luntta, Karl (1991). *Jamaica Handbook*. Chico, CA: Moon Publishers.

Maingot, Anthony P. (1980). "Cuba and the Commonwealth Caribbean: Playing the Cuban card." *Caribbean Review* 9: 7-10, 44-49.

Major, Clarence, ed. (1994). *Juba to Jive: A Dictionary of African-*

American Slang. New York: Penguin Books.

Manley, Michael (1982). "Introduction: Reggae, a revolutionary impulse." In: *Reggae International*, Stephen Davis and Peter Simon, eds. New York: Rogner & Bernhard GMBH, pp. 11-13.

Mason, Clifford (1980). "Waiting on the man." *Geo: A New View of our World* 2(9): 124-146.

Meditz, Sandra W. and Hanratty, Dennis M. (1989). *Islands of the Commonwealth Caribbean: A Regional Study*. Washington, DC: Department of the Army.

Meyer, Downey (1985). Unpublished data from the folder: "Folk Speech — Jamaican." Berkeley, CA: Folklore Archives, University of California.

Mills, Jane (1989). *Womanwords: A Dictionary of Words about Women*. New York: Free Press.

Mühlhäusler, Peter (1979). *Growth and Structure of the Lexicon of New Guinea Pidgin*. Series C, No. 52. Canberra: Pacific Linguistics, Australian National University.

Mulvaney, Rebekah Michele (1990). *Rastafari and Reggae: A Dictionary and Sourcebook.* New York: Greenwood Press.

Nettleford, Rex M. (1970). *Mirror Mirror: Identity, Race and Protest in Jamaica.* Kingston, Jamaica: William Collins and Sangster.

New York City Police Department (1985). "Rasta crime." *Caribbean Review* 14(1): 12-15, 39-40.

Ngũgĩ wa Thiong'o (1986). *Decolonizing the Mind: The Politics of Language in African Literature.* Portsmouth, NH: Heinemann Educational Books.

Nicholas, Tracy (1979). *Rastafari: A Way of Life.* Garden City, New York: Anchor Books.

Owens, Joseph (1976). *Dread: The Rastafarians of Jamaica.* Kingston, Jamaica: Sangster's Book Stores.

Paros, Lawrence (1984). *The Erotic Tongue: A Sexual Lexicon.* New York: Henry Holt.

Partridge, Eric (1984). *A Dictionary of Slang and Unconventional English: Colloquialisms and*

Catch-phrases Solecisms and Catachreses Nicknames and Vulgarisms. Paul Beal, ed. New York: Macmillan.

Partridge, Eric (1989 [1950]). *A Dictionary of the Underworld*. Hertfordshire, Great Britain: Routledge & Kegan Paul.

Patterson, Orlando (1964). *The Children of Sisyphus*. Harlow, England: Longman.

Pauwels, Marcel (1951). "Le culte de Nyabingi (Ruanda)." *Anthropos* 46: 337-357.

Pollard, Velma (1982). "The social history of Dread Talk." *Caribbean Quarterly* 28(4): 17-40.

Pollard, Velma (1983). "The social history of Dread Talk." In: *Studies in Caribbean Language*. Lawrence D. Carrington, ed. St. Augustine, Trinidad: Society for Caribbean Linguistics, pp. 46-62.

Pollard, Velma (1984). "Word sounds: The language of Rastafari in Barbados and St. Lucia." *Jamaica Journal* 17(1): 57-62.

Pollard, Velma (1985). "Dread Talk — the speech of the Rastafarian in Jamaica." *Rastafari.* Kingston,

91

Jamaica: Caribbean Quarterly, University of the West Indies, pp. 32-41.

Pollard, Velma (1986). "Innovation in Jamaican Creole. The speech of Rastafari." In: *Varieties of English Around the World: Focus on the Caribbean*, Manfred Görlach and John A. Holm, eds., Vol. 8. Philadelphia: John Benjamins Publishing, pp. 157-166.

Pollard, Velma (1990). Personal communication.

Redfern, Walter (1984). *Puns*. New York: Basil Blackwell.

Roberts, Peter A. (1988). *West Indians and Their Language*. New York: Cambridge University Press.

Sanders, Rory (1982). "From the root of King David." In: *Reggae International*, Stephen Davis and Peter Simon, eds. New York: Rogner & Bernhard GMBH, pp. 59-68.

Schwartz, Theodore (1962). "The Paliau Movement in the Admiralty Islands, 1946-1954." *Anthropological Papers of the American Museum of Natural History* 49(2): 211-421.

Sheridan, Maureen (1987). "Peter Tosh: The last words and violent death of a reggae hero." *Musician* 100: 21, 22, 24, 26, 28, 30, 40, 121.

Simpson, George Eaton (1980). *Religious Cults of the Caribbean: Trinidad, Jamaica and Haiti.* Río Piedras, Puerto Rico: Institute of Caribbean Studies, University of Puerto Rico, 3rd ed.

Sims Holt, Grace (1972). "'Inversion' in Black communication." In: *Rappin' and Stylin' Out: Communication in Urban Black America,* Thomas Kochman, ed. Chicago: University of Illinois Press, pp. 152-159.

Smith, M.G.; Augier, Roy; and Nettleford, Rex (1978 [1960]). *The Rastafari Movement in Kingston, Jamaica.* Mona, Jamaica: University of the West Indies.

Sobo, Elisa Janine (1993). *One Blood: The Jamaican Body.* Albany: State University of New York.

Tafari, I. Jabulani (1985). "The Rastafari — successors of Marcus Garvey." *Rastafari.* Kingston, Jamaica: Caribbean Quarterly, University of the West Indies, pp. 1-12. [This is a book reprint of a volume of the *Caribbean Quarterly*]

Tafari, I. Jabulani (1988). "Reggae radix... Peter Tosh." *Reggae Report* 6(1): 18-19, 30, 33, 35-36.

Tannahill, Reay (1975). *Flesh and Blood: A History of the Cannibal Complex.* New York: Dorset Press.

Thelwell, Michael (1980). *The Harder They Come.* New York: Grove Press.

Thrupp, Sylvia L., ed. (1970). *Millennial Dreams in Action: Studies in Revolutionary Religious Movements.* New York: Shocken Books.

Todd, Loreto (1974). *Pidgins and Creoles.* London: Routledge & Kegan Paul.

Waters, Anita M. (1985). *Race, Class, and Political Symbols: Rastafari and Reggae in Jamaican Politics.* New Brunswick, New Jersey: Transaction Books.

Wentworth, Harold and Flexner, Stuart Berg (1975). *Dictionary of American Slang*, 2nd ed. New York: Thomas Y. Crowell.

White, Timothy (1989). *Catch a Fire: The Life of Bob Marley.* New York: Henry Holt.

Wolynski, Mara; Schine, Cathleen; Mayo, Anna; Moroz, Josh; Trilling, Roger; Weston, Bradford; and Whitcraft, Teri. (1978). "Illegalize It." *The Village Voice* 23(42): 28.

Yawney, Carole D. (1976). "Remnants of all nations: Rastafarian attitudes to race and nationality." In: *Ethnicity in the Americas.* Frances Henry, ed. Hague: Mouton, pp. 231-262.

Yawney, Carole D. (1979a). *Lions in Babylon: The Rastafarians of Jamaica as a Visionary Movement.* Ph.D. Thesis: McGill University.

Yawney, Carole D. (1979b). "Dread wasteland: Rastafarian ritual in West Kingston, Jamaica." *Occasional Publications in Anthropology, Ethnology Series. University of North Colorado*, no. 33, pp. 154-178.

About the Author

Thomas H. Slone is a staff scientist at the University of California at Berkeley, where he has published more than 30 papers in the field of cancer research over the past 17 years. He has traveled extensively, and has visited Iindonesia five times.

He has translated and edited a monumental two-volume collection of Papua New Guinean folktales, *One Thousand One Papua New Guinean Nights*. He has written the article, "Tok nogut: An introduction to malediction in Papua New Guinea" (*Maledicta: The International Journal of Verbal Aggression* 11: 75-104, 1996), and he is a major contributor to a revision of a Tok Pisin-English dictionary.

Masalai Press

Masalai Press is a publisher specializing in Pacific Island and Asian folklore. Other titles published by Masalai Press are:

- *One Thousand One Papua New Guinean Nights: Folktales from Wantok Newspaper. Volume 1: Tales from 1972-1985.* Edited and translated by Thomas H. Slone. 528 pages, 8-1/4 by 11 inches. ISBN 0-9714127-0-7.
- *One Thousand One Papua New Guinean Nights: Folktales Stories from Wantok Newspaper. Volume 2: Tales from 1986-1997, Indices, Glossary, References, and Maps.* Edited and translated by Thomas H. Slone. 613 pages, 8-1/4 by 11 inches. ISBN 0-9714127-1-5.
- *Prokem: An Analysis of a Jakartan Slang,* by Thomas H. Slone, 108 pages, 5 by 8 inches. ISBN 0-9714127-5-8.

Masalai Press takes its name from the malevolent spirits of Papua New Guinea. These spirits can be associated with a specific location (such as a mountain) or specific natural feature (such as a whirlpool). In a human-like (anthropomorphic) form, a *masalai* is often a large and/or ugly cannibal, similar to an ogre.